Original title:
The Sonnets of Saturn

Copyright © 2025 Creative Arts Management OÜ
All rights reserved.

Author: Sophia Kingsley
ISBN HARDBACK: 978-1-80567-760-4
ISBN PAPERBACK: 978-1-80567-881-6

Rhapsodies of the Frozen Storm

In chilly space where snowflakes giggle,
The stars do dance and comets wiggle.
A frozen grin on Saturn's face,
Making jokes in a boundless place.

With rings that jingle like silver bells,
They tease the planets, oh how it dwells!
A snowman made of alien goo,
Winks at Mars, saying, "Join the crew!"

In winter's grip, the moons do play,
With cosmic frisbees of ice today.
Laughter echoes through the void,
As Jupiter smiles, quite overjoyed.

Yet when the sun peeks out to shine,
The frozen jesters make a line.
They warm their jokes in golden rays,
And laugh at Saturn's icy ways.

Strands of Light in Cosmic Weavings

In the fabric of the night so bright,
There are strands of giggles and pure delight.
With cosmic threads of happiness spun,
Silly tales of races won.

A comet's tail trails like a kite,
Dodging asteroids with all its might.
While aliens sip on glittery tea,
Shouting, "Catch me if you can, you see!"

Wobbling planets, they jump and twirl,
Creating chaos in a cosmic whirl.
Their rings all tangled with cosmic yarn,
Sending Saturn into a funny barn.

So join the stars in their colorful glee,
Where every beam sings, "Come dance with me!"
In this vast theater, jokes take flight,
As laughter echoes through the starry night.

A Journey Through Galactic Gaze

In the night, stars laugh and tease,
Planets play hide and seek with ease.
Comets zoom with a silly grin,
Asteroids dance, letting chaos begin.

Galaxies twirl in a goofy jive,
Space-time tickles, feels so alive.
With every leap, we bounce and sway,
A chuckle echoes, come what may.

The Cosmic Ballad of Wanderers

Wanderers roam with gleeful quests,
Singing songs of cosmic jest.
They trip on stardust, giggle and fall,
In the vastness, joy stands tall.

Uranus spins with a cheeky tease,
While Saturn's rings spin like a breeze.
We chase a moonbeam, what a sight,
Dancing through darkness, pure delight.

Spectrums of Color in a Lunar Waltz

Lunar lights shimmer with vibrant hues,
Dancing shadows play, in playful views.
Colors collide in a silly spree,
As Martian dust joins in for free.

Neon comets flash, a show so bright,
While Venus twirls in a gown of light.
We giggle at dreams that float and sway,
In this lunar waltz, we laugh and play.

Harmonies of the Whispering Stars

Stars whisper secrets with a wink,
They tease the moon, don't you think?
In a symphony of joy we bask,
As cosmic riddles prompt us to ask.

Planets hum tunes, silly and sweet,
In a galactic choir, we feel the beat.
Laughter rings out, a universal jest,
We dance among orbs; we're truly blessed.

A Dance Among the Moons

In the sky, the moons do sway,
Cartwheeling madly night and day.
One tripped on dust from an old star,
And yelled, "Look out! Here comes my car!"

Jupiter laughed with mighty glee,
Said, "Join my band, come dance with me!"
Mars wore boots, a dapper sight,
While Pluto laughed at their delight.

A comet zoomed, a flash of light,
While asteroids laughed at their flight.
With twinkling eyes, they spun around,
In this cosmic dance, they were crowned!

But then they tripped, oh what a scene,
Moons and planets in a twisty routine.
With giggles echoing through the void,
A jolly toast to fun enjoyed!

Starlit Confessions

Underneath a sky so wide,
Stars began to chat and bide.
"I wish I had a cooler name!"
Said one who thought he was to blame.

Another star with a twinkle bright,
Declared, "I'm known for my great height!"
While a dwarf star chuckled low,
"At least my friends don't shine, you know!"

They shared tales of comets fast,
And how their fame was often cast.
"I once was a supernova, it's true!"
Said one, "Now I'm just a sparkly blue!"

As they laughed, a meteor flew by,
"Hey, remember me? I was sky high!"
With quirky jokes, they shone till dawn,
Starlit confessions, their woes were gone!

Gravity's Embrace

Gravity pulled them close with glee,
Making planets cringe, most definitely.
"Stop it, Earth! You're too clingy!"
"Let's dance," said Mars, feeling zingy.

Saturn sighed with her rings so bright,
"They're heavy, I can't levitate tonight!"
Venus laughed, swirling in space,
"Quit your whining, it's all just a race!"

They crowded near, a cosmic pile,
With pull and push, they joked a while.
"Hey, Moon, could you lighten the load?"
"Only if you share your abode!"

And thus they wandered in a spin,
While giggles and chirps made them grin.
Gravity's embrace, a jovial phase,
Dancing together in playful ways!

The Poet's Rings

In the depths of space, a poet sighed,
"Rings of Saturn! I'll be your guide!"
With quill in hand, such tales to spin,
"A dance of worlds! Let's begin!"

Each ring a rhyme, a playful line,
Filled with giggles, bright and fine.
"Oh, how I wish to be a star!"
"Stay grounded, friend, and play guitar!"

A meteor came, stole the scene,
"Where's the punchline? I want some cream!"
With laughter echoing through the void,
The poet scribbled, feeling buoyed.

As the dance of planets twirled and spun,
Fiction and fact could join the fun.
From cosmic heights, to Earth's embrace,
The poet's rings brought smiles to space!

Rings of Time

In the sky, so far away,
Rings of dust and ice do play.
One looks like a fancy hula hoop,
While aliens cheer in a cosmic group.

Time ticks slow, or so they say,
While Saturn spins the night away.
With gas so thick, it can confound,
The best-laid plans never found.

Saturn's moons are quite the crowd,
Gossiping stars are often loud.
They throw a party, light-years apart,
Sipping on stardust, making art.

Watch out for that space cow!
He's dancing low, but oh, the wow!
With rings to twirl, he'd steal the show,
In this galactic rodeo!

Whispers from the Outer Realm

A comet passing, bright and bold,
Whispers secrets yet untold.
"Hey, Martians! Send us your best!"
"Slow your roll, and take a rest!"

The stars gossip, quite the scene,
One twinkling like a jellybean.
Galaxies giggle, tumbling bright,
In the chaos of cosmic night.

Uranus joins in, with an eye roll,
"Stop your whining, let's take a stroll!"
Jupiter, jolly, shouts from afar,
"Pass me that drink, you moonlit star!"

Awkward silence from Neptune's crew,
"What's the matter? Did we lose you?"
Then Saturn laughs, spins with glee,
"Come back, join our little spree!"

Celestial Love Letters

Roses are red, violets are blue,
Written in stardust, a love so true.
Cosmic Cupid with a wink and a sigh,
Sending sweet nothings from way up high.

Moons writing notes, full of charm,
Hoping their crush won't come to harm.
"Hey, Saturn! You're looking quite fine,
Can we meet where the stars align?"

Starlit hearts dance across the night,
With comets swooping in delight.
Mars blushes, "Oops! Did I trip?"
Finding love in a rocket ship.

Letters in space, lost in the breeze,
Hoping to charm all the cosmic bees.
"Meet me at noon, where the sun will shine,
Or perhaps at dusk, under the pine!"

Echoes in the Void

Floating softly, the echoes call,
In that vast space, they bounce and fall.
"Is anybody there?" shouts one tiny star,
But the silence replies, "Not from afar!"

Alien radio, blaring fun tunes,
Dancing alone with those funky moons.
When a supernova throws a grand ball,
The shy little planets can't help but stall.

Bouncing echoes and silly laughs,
Space-time pranks, like cosmic gaffes.
"Did you hear that?" says a comet, quite bold,
"I think I found Mars, or was it just cold?"

In the void where the funny things lie,
Even vacuumed silence can flutter and fly.
So, join the chaos, don't stay aloof,
Let the echoes carry your cosmic goof!

Visions from an Ancient Sky

Stars burst like popcorn,
Chasing the moon's old game.
They dance in awkward orbits,
How silly they must feel.

A comet sneezed last night,
Sending sparks across the dark.
Planets giggled, spun around,
Creating a cosmic lark.

Galaxies wear funny hats,
Flipping through the stellar sea.
They boast of all their riches,
Yet they're just swirling debris.

Cosmic clowns in endless play,
Juggling time with comical flair.
In this vast, wacky universe,
Every skit's a cosmic dare.

Reflections on the Turbulent Winds

Winds howl like laughing children,
Tickling the edges of stars.
They whip through the galaxies,
Waving goodbye to Mars.

Nebulas puff like cheeks,
Blowing pastel-colored puffs.
They whisper secrets of laughter,
While dancing through cosmic bluffs.

Space dust kicks up with glee,
As meteors race past in a blur.
Comets argue about direction,
Which way to spin and stir.

In turbulence, there's joy found,
In every zippy, zany move.
The universe twirls and tumbles,
In a rhythm that can't help but groove.

A Tapestry of Cosmic Echos

Stars weave a fabric of chuckles,
Each stitch a twinkling tease.
Galaxies giggle in patterns,
Spinning tales in the breeze.

A nebula, puffy and bright,
Fabricates clouds of delight.
Every echo a joke shared,
In the canvas of the night.

Echoes bounce like rubber balls,
Through the vastness of delight.
Making rhythms of laughter,
In the silence of the night.

A quilt of cosmic humor,
Stitched with love from the past.
Each twinkle, a tale of whimsy,
In the universe's cast.

Navigating the Celestial Currents

Sailing on solar breezes,
Navigating giggles and grins.
Charting courses through the stars,
Where silly wisdom begins.

A planet's wobbly pirouette,
Leads to laughter in the void.
Cosmic winds are playful sprites,
With every burden enjoyed.

Starlight winks through the chaos,
As comets race in a line.
Navigators of the far skies,
Share jokes over cups of wine.

Each journey a playful romp,
In the universe's embrace.
With laughter as our compass,
We find joy in every space.

Shadows of the Distant World

In twilight's laugh, the shadows play,
Their jig is wiggly, come what may.
A comet trips on laughing stars,
While space-time giggles, 'Aren't we bizarre?'

The moons are juggling teal and gold,
While asteroids tell tales so bold.
Each planet grins with cheeky flair,
In cosmic jokes, they love to share.

Bright rings of laughter spin around,
As they tumble, never touch the ground.
From icy realms to fiery lanes,
Galactic glee in joyful chains.

When distant worlds all come to play,
The milky way becomes a ballet.
Gravity's a slippery friend,
In this weird realm, the fun won't end.

Tides of Celestial Longing

The waves of stars, they ebb and flow,
With cosmic wit, they steal the show.
A supernova's catchy beat,
Makes even black holes tap their feet.

In Neptune's sea, the laughter swirls,
Where fish in hats do secret twirls.
With glimmers shimmering, oh-so-bright,
They dance through nebulae each night.

The satellites in constant spin,
Join in the ruckus, let the fun begin.
With a splash of light from every hue,
These tides of joy are fresh and new.

A starlit tide, it pulls us near,
To share a smile, to feel no fear.
In waves of wonder, let's all sway,
While laughter carries us away.

Enchanted by Gaseous Whirls

In rings of gas, the giggles bloom,
With spicy winds that push and zoom.
Each puff of laughter fills the space,
Creating chaos with endless grace.

A swirling cloud of colors bright,
Does cartwheels in the velvet night.
With meteor showers giggling past,
The humor flows, and joys amass.

Beware the jesters of the sky,
Who juggle planets as they fly.
In this celestial masquerade,
The echoes of their fun won't fade.

Together they spin, oh what a sight,
These gaseous whirlwinds bring delight.
Forever twirling in cosmic play,
In laughter's grip, they'll always stay.

Dreams in a Celestial Sphere

In dreams where stars are made of cheese,
The galaxies wobble with such ease.
Jupiter does a silly dance,
While Saturn waves with a twinkling glance.

The visions spin like toddler carts,
Through paintbrush worlds with joyful hearts.
Each dreamer laughs in cosmic cheer,
As colors burst and disappear.

From moonlit glades to comet trails,
Imagination never fails.
In cosmos bright, the humor beams,
These hefty dreams are filled with schemes.

In a sphere where nothing seems quite true,
The laughter finds its way to you.
With cosmic giggles all around,
In such sweet dreams, we are unbound.

Eternal Whispers of the Night

In the dark, the stars do giggle,
As a comet passes, doing a wiggle.
The moon wears shades, looks rather coy,
While planets play tag, oh what a joy!

Whispers float on cosmic breeze,
Aliens dance with interstellar ease.
A black hole burps, with a cheeky grin,
And all the cosmos joins in with a spin.

Asteroids waltz on a merry path,
While Jupiter laughs in its gas-filled bath.
Galactic jesters, they roam the night,
Tickling each nebula just out of sight.

Eternal whispers beneath the stars,
Jokes told by moons, no need for cars.
The universe chuckles, oh what a sight,
As starlit tales unfold in delight.

Whispers of Celestial Rings

In the rings of a giant, a squirrel takes a ride,
Spinning and flipping with cosmic pride.
Saturn's bands toss confetti of ice,
As moons play hopscotch, oh isn't it nice?

Uranus snickers, it's tickled and bold,
While Neptune's secrets are better untold.
The stardust dancers twirl with flair,
As comets join in without a care.

Rings of laughter echo through space,
Each satellite grinning, a merry face.
Cosmic tickles make gas giants sway,
In a whirl of delight, they laugh and play.

Whispers travel, a giggle parade,
Through Saturn's rings, where joy never fades.
Celestial jokes in a stellar spree,
As the universe chuckles, wild and free.

Ballad of the Cosmic Voyager

A spaceship zooms past a laughing star,
With a cosmic navigator, oh what a czar!
Planets wave, with a giggle so grand,
As they toss tiny comets, like grains of sand.

Orbiting moons send a wink so sly,
While meteoroids dance in the endless sky.
The voyager hums a merry tune,
Chasing black holes beneath the moon.

Galactic winds play a symphony bright,
As quarks take flight with pure delight.
An interstellar journey filled with glee,
With cosmic giggles for all to see.

In the void of space, where laughter's the rule,
Stars gather 'round, each one a fool.
Through endless routes, the traveler sings,
A ballad of joy, where the universe swings.

Echoes in the Particle Storm

A storm brews up with a comedic twist,
Particles zipping through a cosmic mist.
Twirling like dancers, they laugh and play,
In a whirl of giggles that brightens the day.

Photons bounce like jesters in glee,
As the universe winks at you and me.
Echoes of laughter dance in the dark,
While quirks and quarks perform in the spark.

The chaos of atoms, a carnival scene,
Where every collision is oddly serene.
Gravity tickles, and neutrinos tease,
While laughter resounds through the cosmic breeze.

In this playful storm, where jokes never die,
Let's celebrate wonders as they whirl by.
With each little echo, a smile takes form,
In the quirky embrace of the particle storm.

Sagas of the Cosmic Twilight

In cosmic dance, the stars may prance,
A comet slips, and takes a chance.
Planets giggle, spin and twirl,
While asteroids debate, 'Who's got the pearl?'

Black holes laugh, they take a bite,
Swallowing light, oh what a sight!
Galaxies sip from stardust cups,
Before they toast and hiccup up.

Aliens tickle and tease their pets,
With cosmic fish in strange new nets.
They pull a prank on Jupiter's moon,
Saying, "Dance, you rock, or you'll get pruned!"

In twilight's glow, the jokes unfold,
As space-time weaves stories bold.
So grab a seat, hold onto your hats,
For the universe is full of spats!

Whirlwinds of Time and Space

In whirlwinds bright, the comets weave,
Time trips on light, oh what a reprieve!
Time lags behind, in a tickle fight,
While space plays peekaboo, out of sight.

Planets race, in a cosmic game,
Mars is bold, but Saturn's to blame!
"Stop spinning so fast!" the Earth does cry,
"I'm dizzy enough, oh my, oh my!"

Time twists its mustache and takes a stroll,
Winking at stars, with its fluffy soul.
The Milky Way chuckles, full of delight,
As supernovae pop in the night!

Oh, the humor wrapped in this cosmic spree,
With time and space, it's a fun jamboree.
Join the ride, let laughter ensue,
In whirlwinds where giggles float like dew!

Hallowed Words of the Celestial

In sacred scripts, the stars do scribble,
With ancient tales that make us giggle.
A pulsar jokes, "I blink, I shine!
But quiz me on math? That's crossing the line!"

Nebulas whisper, oh what a crowd,
Telling secrets both soft and loud.
"Did you hear of the black hole's feast?
It swallowed the moon, said it was a beast!"

Celestial beings, with halos so bright,
Tumble and topple in cosmic light.
With humor profound, like a cosmic bard,
They twirl and tease, leaving us charred!

So listen well, to their hallowed words,
Where laughter and joy dance like birds.
In this celestial choir, don't be shy,
Join in the laughter, let your spirit fly!

Adventures in the Nebula's Heart

In the nebula's heart, a joke takes flight,
Stars play poker, oh what a sight!
"Full house!" cries one, with light-years of glee,
While the cosmos deals cards, oh so carefree.

Planets unite, for a dance-off grand,
With twinkling lights, they take a stand.
"Watch my moves!" beams a gas giant proud,
While moons spin dizzy, beneath the crowd.

Comets race, in a jesting chase,
While asteroids laugh, just a little misplaced.
"Caution!" they shout, "Don't crash the party!"
But who can resist? It's all so hearty!

In the heart of the nebula, fun galore,
With silly antics and cosmic lore.
So join the revels, let your spirit dart,
For in this adventure, there's joy to impart!

Verses of the Ethereal Wind

In the cosmos, a breeze went by,
Tickling stars as they winked an eye.
Planets giggled in their merry spin,
While comets raced, shouting, "Let's begin!"

A moonbeam slipped, oh what a sight,
Tripped over Venus, causing a fright.
Galaxies twinkled, saying, "Oh dear!"
As space dust danced without any fear.

Gleams of Light in Celestial Gravitations

Jupiter laughed, with a jolly tone,
"Why so serious? Just float and moan!"
Nebulas painted their colors bright,
While stardust sprinkled a sparkly light.

A shooting star with a silly grin,
Fell past a black hole with quite a spin.
"Catch me if you can!" it called aloud,
Spinning around like a boisterous crowd.

Catching Dreams in Astral Currents

Dreamers drifted on soft space waves,
Whispering wishes, oh how it craves!
Asteroids chuckled, "We're on a roll!"
As their rocky hearts twinkled bright as coal.

A galaxy's giggle echoed afar,
Tickled by light from a nearby star.
"Let's play tag!" the dark matter yelled,
Chasing comets where laughter swelled.

Reveries of the Cosmic Dance

In the ballroom of the night sky's grace,
Stars twirled around in a dazzling chase.
Mercury stomped with a beat so spry,
While Saturn swayed, tipping its eye.

A dance-off erupted, oh what delight!
With meteors leaping, igniting the night.
While cosmic beings juggled black holes,
Sharing chuckles and whimsical roles.

Eternal Lullabies of the Cosmos

In a night sky filled with stars,
Planets play their silly guitars.
They twirl and dance with glowing grace,
While comets giggle in endless space.

The moon spins tales of bedtime cheer,
While meteors whiz, oh so near!
Each orbit brings a brand new joke,
As stardust bursts from a laughing smoke.

A cosmic band plays out of tune,
Serenading bright the sleepy moon.
Galaxy whispers, dreams take flight,
In this waltz of twilight delight.

So lean back, let the universe sing,
Join in laughter, let your heart swing.
In this lullaby of cosmic glee,
The stars ensure sweet dreams for thee.

Echoes from the Rings' Embrace

Rings of laughter spin around,
As Saturn prances, joy unbound.
Its moons all giggle, round and round,
In that cosmic circus, fun is found.

A comet sneezes, stars too bright,
Planets chuckle at the sight.
Stardust tickles with every glide,
Cosmic jesters bouncing side to side.

The gas giants play hide-and-seek,
While asteroids wobble, quite unique.
Bursting laughter from every space,
In this arena, joy finds its place.

So let those echoes swirl and sway,
In the dance of night and day.
With each twinkle, a wink is shared,
For in this galaxy, none is spared.

Tales of Celestial Migrations

Across the sky, they roam and play,
Starry travelers on their way.
With every leap, a story told,
Of cosmic pranks both shy and bold.

Nebulas whisper jokes so bright,
While comets laugh in agile flight.
Planets call from rings so wide,
Sharing secrets, side by side.

They sail through time, with mischief grand,
Sketching constellations in a band.
Galaxies twirl, a cosmic spree,
Their laughter echoes endlessly.

So wander on, dear stellar crew,
In every journey, find what's true.
With humor spanning light-years long,
In this universe, we all belong.

Shadows Across the Stellar Expanse

Shadows whisper on cosmic waves,
As stardust frolics in its caves.
In silence, shadows play a game,
Beneath bright galaxies, none the same.

From black holes out to comets' tails,
Dancing jokes ride on the gales.
A supernova bursts in glee,
Lighting up the vast marquee.

Nebulas craft a funny mask,
In the dark, they love to bask.
In every flicker, laughter shines,
Across the void, where humor twines.

So as you gaze at heavens wide,
Let the starlight be your guide.
For in the shadows, joy is cast,
And cosmic fun will always last.

Fantasies from the Ringed Wonder

In a world where pizza flies,
Aliens wear silly ties.
They dance on Saturn's icy rings,
Twirling to the sounds of zing!

Jellybeans rain from the sky,
As comet tails begin to fly.
Saturn's moons host disco balls,
With funky grooves that bounce and enthrall.

The space cows jump over the night,
Milking stardust, oh what a sight!
They moo in rhythms soft and sweet,
While astronauts do the moonwalk beat.

A jump rope made of cosmic rays,
Invites the stars for endless plays.
Galactic gnomes plant silly seeds,
In gardens where imagination leads.

Timeless Echoes Beyond the Sphere

In orbit, time skips like a stone,
Where cosmic trips feel like home.
Planets giggle, comets cheer,
As fun galore brings laughter near.

An octopus wears funky shades,
And juggles planets, none are fazed.
With rings so thick, they double take,
As space-time bends for giggles' sake.

Radio waves hum tunes so bright,
Telling tales of midnight light,
Hello to Martians, they reply,
With jokes about a pumpkin pie.

Shooting stars race for the prize,
In a contest of laughter and lies.
The universe spins with cosmic charm,
As echoes ring without alarm.

The Language of the Stars

Stars gossip in a twinkly hum,
While meteors play on a cosmic drum.
The language of laughter fills the air,
With ticklish nebulae everywhere.

Comets trade secrets in a waltz,
Their tails tickle the Milky Way's vaults.
Jovian giants wear oversized shoes,
And chuckle at Saturnian views.

With whispers loud enough to hear,
Galactic giggles draw stars near.
Words float like bubbles in the void,
A cosmic joke, never destroyed.

Every black hole has its own punchline,
Pulling jokes that seem so fine.
In the expanse where humor thrives,
The universe laughs as long as it survives.

Illuminated Thoughts in Darkness

In the dark, where shadows gleam,
Funny thoughts float like a dream.
Lightbulb stars flash with delight,
As cosmic clowns prance in the night.

A space whale sings a silly tune,
Dancing 'neath the cheeky moon.
While meteor showers paint the sky,
With colors that make the crickets sigh.

Galaxies spin with graceful flair,
Chasing comets without a care.
Whimsical tales from light-years away,
Bring smiles and laughter to our day.

In the vastness of the void, we find,
Jokes are woven, intertwined.
Illuminated thoughts bring a spark,
Lighting giggles all through the dark.

Lament of the Gaseous Giant

In the sky, I twist and sway,
Belly full of gas all day.
Floating rings that catch the light,
What a sight, what a fright!

Down below, the moons all grin,
Chasing tail, they join the spin.
I've lost track of where I float,
Watch out now, here comes my coat!

Meteor showers joke and tease,
Bouncing 'round like it's a breeze.
But when I burp, oh what a sound,
Echoes bounce, my friends all drown!

Oh to be a solid rock,
Instead of this ol' gaseous stock.
I dance and whirl, a cosmic show,
With endless laughs and room to blow!

Dances in the Twilight Orbit

In twilight's glow, I jig and prance,
Twinkling stars, come join my dance!
Spinning fast, I trip and fall,
Whoops! Watch out, I hit a wall!

Comets whirl with a cheeky grin,
Rocket trails leave hints of sin.
Satellites clapping in delight,
Who'll take home the dance-off night?

A moonlit sombrero on my head,
Twisting through the cosmic spread.
With every step, a joyful cheer,
Making friends is why I'm here!

At last I bow, the crowd erupts,
Sending waves that bounce and plump.
With every crunch, and every squeal,
This twilight dance is quite a deal!

Melodies of the Ethereal Realm

Softest tunes float through the air,
Cosmic whispers everywhere.
Plucking stars like guitar strings,
Oh, the joy that laughter brings!

I serenade the drifting dust,
In raucous rhymes, I place my trust.
Each note, a bubble, burst with glee,
Floating high, come sing with me!

But beware, a misstep here
Could send me spiraling, oh dear!
A symphony of giggles churns,
As one by one, the planet turns.

So let us hum this jovial tune,
Beneath the shining silver moon.
Shall we waltz 'neath starlit skies?
The cosmic jokes, they never die!

Rhapsody on a Planetly Whirl

On a swirl where laughter roams,
I spin and dance to dreamy gnomes.
Poking fun at bits of rock,
With swirling skirts they love to shock!

Gravity laughs, a pulling jest,
Tugging at me, like all the rest.
I'm the center of such a swirl,
Sending off a twirling twirl!

Asteroids toss like clumsy jesters,
Splitting seams and cracked investors.
While I whirl in dizzy glee,
Let's break out for a galaxy tea!

So join this raucous planetary play,
Where laughs and orbits spin away.
With cosmic quirks and starry grace,
I find my joy in this vast space!

Vignettes of the Galactic Voyage

In a ship made of candy, we zoom through the stars,
With jellybean engines and chocolate bars.
Asteroids bounce like rubbery balls,
While space cows moo from their cosmic stalls.

A comet waved with a sparkly tail,
But forgot to ask for a sturdy sail.
We tossed back snacks from our gumball stash,
Giggles erupted with every flash.

We spun like tops in a cosmic dance,
Dodging moonbeams in an interstellar prance.
A space crab clapped with an electric cheer,
As we toasted with sodas, the funniest beer!

Oh, the quirks of our voyage across the night,
In a universe painted with laughter and light.
With stars as our friends, we're never alone,
On this silly adventure we've whimsically flown.

Poems from the Nebula's Heart

Floating in clouds made of candy floss,
Where socks become ships and pillows, the gloss.
The stars giggle softly, whispering jokes,
While comets throw parties with dancing folks.

A nebula painted in colors so bright,
Is hosting a feast of interstellar delight.
We slurped up the stardust with fresh lemonade,
While planets all joined in a cosmic parade.

A sly little elf with a cap and a wand,
Conjured up puddles of sparkling fond.
We slipped and we slid on the silvery trails,
As the moon gave applause with its crescent wails.

In this circus of stars, the fun never wanes,
With laughter and joy flowing through our veins.
A jester in orbit spins tales full of cheer,
In the heart of the nebula, life's nothing but clear.

Light Dances on Rings of Time

Around and around, the light likes to twirl,
On rings of color, it gives a whirl.
Planets wear hats, quite silly and tall,
While ukeleles echo in the cosmic hall.

Tickling the stars with a radiant beam,
As laughter erupts in a comet's sweet dream.
Jupiter joins with a grin that's so wide,
Sending balloons on a light-speed ride.

The shadows giggle when darkness takes flight,
As photons play tag in the soft, starry night.
Orbits collide in a wobbly dance,
With stardust confetti, we all take a chance.

So let's toast to time, that mischievous sprite,
Whirling and swirling in the glow of night.
With cheers to the moments that make our hearts shine,
As light dances onward, through the fabric of time.

The Gravity of Distant Whispers

In a realm where gravity plays silly tricks,
Whispers of stardust pull us into clicks.
The cosmos chuckles with each little pluck,
As we float on laughter, just hoping for luck.

Shooting stars giggle, sharing secrets so bright,
While black holes spin tales that vanish from sight.
We twirl in the waves of a gentle embrace,
As the universe tickles us all in this space.

A moonbeam suggests we hold hands and glide,
In this whimsical dance, we slide side by side.
Nebulas whisper sweet nothings to trees,
As planets conspire to mess with the breeze.

So here's to the whispers that make us all smile,
With joy in the cosmos, let's stay for a while.
For in the grand scheme of this funny ballet,
The gravity pulls us in magical ways.

Whirls of Time Around an Orb

Round and round the planets spin,
Time slips out, a cheeky grin.
Tick-tock goes the cosmic clock,
Who needs a watch? Just a sock!

Galaxies dance in a waltz,
Everyone's smiling, no faults.
Stars crack jokes, light-years away,
Laughter echoes, hip-hip-hooray!

Gravity's game, oh what a hoot,
Falling gently, in zero suit.
Round we go, on this giant ride,
Cosmic carnival, let's collide!

Planets play tag, don't be late,
Comets race, they can't wait.
Hop on board, it's time to twirl,
In the universe, we laugh and swirl!

Ridges of Ice and Gales Unseen

On icy peaks, where snowflakes jest,
The winds whisper secrets, they know best.
Penguins slide down with a giggly cheer,
In this chilly kingdom, fun's always near.

Gales blow strong, but do they care?
They toss snowflakes with flair in the air.
Icicles dangle, glimmer and shine,
Like nature's glitter, oh so divine!

Frosty air and a snowball fight,
Laughter rings out, what pure delight!
With a whoosh, here goes a flake,
Oops! Missed the target, oh for Pete's sake!

Icebound giggles, frostbitten smiles,
Each chilly corner holds laughs for miles.
Nature's playground, frozen yet free,
Ridges of ice, where joy's the key!

Songs from the Horizon of Infinity

Horizon hums a silly tune,
As stars boogie to the moon.
Chasing comets, they can't slow,
In this vastness, gleeful woe!

Notes from galaxies, loud and spry,
Strum the strings of the midnight sky.
Echoing laughter, a cosmic choir,
Each twinkling light, a happy flyer!

Melodies drift on solar winds,
Inviting all, the fun begins.
Triangles wobble in stellar dance,
Who knew space had such flair and romance?

Songs of joy, from far-off spheres,
Rippling through the void, no fears.
In laughter's embrace, we'll play on high,
With cosmic rhythms and pies in the sky!

Secrets Beneath Heaven's Veil

Underneath the sky's grand cloak,
Hide little jests and starry folk.
Winking stars tell tales so sly,
As the sun yawns, 'Oh my, oh my!'

Heaven's veil twinkles, a secret code,
Whispers of laughter across the road.
Moonbeams giggle, tickle the trees,
Nature's jesters, riding the breeze.

In shadows deep, where stardust plays,
Mischievous sprites light up the days.
Their fun-filled pranks, a cosmic spree,
Playing hide and seek, just let it be!

Secrets exchanged in the night's embrace,
Laughter echoes in this joyous space.
With each twinkle, a chuckle prevails,
Unveiling life behind heaven's veils!

The Language of Rings

In a realm of floating rocks,
Where no one wears socks,
Planets play a cosmic game,
Saturn's rings call out a name.

Jokes bounce off the icy trails,
Whispers of interstellar tales,
Cosmic chuckles, dancing light,
Strange humor in the night.

Giant gas, oh what a sight,
With stripes that make clowns take flight,
Rings that smile and wink with flair,
A party held in chilly air.

Tickled moons spin 'round and round,
In this jest, joy is found,
With laughter echoing through space,
A whimsical, starry embrace.

Harmonies in the Abyss

In the depths where darkness hums,
Where every silence awkwardly strums,
Bubbles rise with a silly squawk,
Even shadows here can talk.

Echoes laugh through the thick haze,
Making fun of cosmic ways,
Galaxies join in with a tune,
Dancing like a light-hearted loon.

Oh, the stars, what a ruckus they make,
With harmonies that tickle and shake,
In the vast, endless space they spin,
Who knew the void could wear a grin?

Silly sounds drift near the jets,
As planets share their cosmic bets,
In this abyss, joy takes a stand,
With humor as boundless as the land.

Visions Beyond the Horizon

Glimmers dance at the edge of sight,
Possibilities bright as twilight,
Daring dreams flip and fly,
Painting laughs on the cosmic sky.

What's out there? The planets jest,
Hiding secrets in their quest,
Every comet a laughing face,
Leaving trails in the starry space.

Beyond the waves of time and night,
Ideas shimmer, wild and bright,
Every thought a playful leap,
In visions where wonders creep.

Here, the universe spills its cheer,
Whiskers of stardust drawing near,
And as horizons stretch and bend,
Cosmic giggles never end.

Celestial Conversations

In the quiet of the night so still,
Stars whisper secrets with a thrill,
Planets swap their funny tales,
Flipping jokes like silky sails.

Asteroids chime with a silly clang,
While comets swoosh and zippers twang,
Cracking smiles among the void,
Where even silence feels overjoyed.

Silly voices in a cosmic chat,
Nibbling on starry titbits, just like that,
Gravity giggles, pulls with glee,
In these chats, how funny we can be!

So when you gaze at night's embrace,
Remember the humor in outer space,
With every star a blooper bright,
Celestial banter fills the night.

Orbital Reveries

In a cosmic café, stars sip on tea,
Jupiter jests, with a belly so free.
Mars tells a joke about rings and a hat,
While Venus blushes, and laughs, 'Oh, that!

Uranus chuckles, with its sideways grin,
Saturn's got bling that makes cats look thin.
Mercury zips by, a blur in the night,
But even he stops for a joke that's just right.

Neptune's the quiet one, lost in his dreams,
While Pluto pouts, "I'm not what it seems."
Galaxies swirl in this cosmic charade,
All join in the fun, no one's ever dismayed.

As comets shoot past with their tails all aglow,
The universe chuckles, and puts on a show.
From nebulae's giggles to black holes' wide grins,
In this stellar circus, everyone's in!

Serenade in the Silent Depths

In the silence of space, a sound starts to grow,
A gassy old giant turns on a new show.
With bubbles and pops, what a riot it brings,
The echoes of laughter from celestial things.

Stars gather 'round, they can't help but chime,
Neptune's off key, but it's all quite sublime.
While comets serenade with their sparkling tails,
Playing pranks on the orbits, their cosmic details.

A moon plays the piano, its craters the keys,
While asteroids dance, swaying gently with ease.
The vacuum holds magic, the cosmos takes flight,
As humor tickles softly through the void of the night.

And as the sun winks with a vibrant delight,
The dark and the light become jolly and bright.
In this vast serenade, humor shall peek,
Amongst the grand wonders of space, so unique!

Reverberations of the Great Beyond

In the great beyond, the echoes collide,
A neutron star laughs, as it takes us for a ride.
Galactic giggles ripple through spacetime,
As black holes snicker, "Now here's the real crime!"

The asteroids tumble, competing in jest,
With meteors visiting, a cosmic quest.
While quasars shine bright, like comedic stars,
They're sending their jokes out to planets and cars.

Constellations chuckle, tracing their lines,
With every new formed galaxy, humor entwines.
In spectral rainbows, the laughter unfolds,
As stardust confetti through space gently rolls.

The universe chuckles, a raucous delight,
Spinning tales of wonder throughout the night.
With light-years of joy wrapping us all tight,
In this echoing dance, everything feels right!

The Dance of Distant Worlds

In a cosmic dance hall, the planets do sway,
Mars leads the line, with a twist and a play.
Jupiter's twirls, like a giant balloon,
While Saturn's rings buzz with a whimsical tune.

Earth's got a rhythm, it shuffles about,
While comets on skates zoom in, then dart out.
Uranus rolls in, with its quirky old style,
Bringing joy to the cosmos, making us smile.

On the dance floor of night, the stars all participate,
With galaxies spinning, they elevate.
The universe winks, in a playful embrace,
As the Milky Way swirls, keeping up with the pace.

So join in the frolic, the endless delight,
In the dance of the worlds, a celestial sight.
With laughter that echoes through the stardust-filled air,
Let's twirl through the cosmos, with style and with flair!

Lanterns in the Cosmic Vastness

In the dark, they glow so bright,
Little lanterns take their flight.
Dancing round the cosmic stew,
Chasing tails like kittens do.

Twinkling lights in a giant bowl,
Stars are just holes with some coal.
Comets slide on banana peels,
Winking at us, oh what deals!

Uranus grins, his rings in a swirl,
While Jupiter spins, giving us a twirl.
Planets giggle, what a show,
Galactic friends in a comical flow.

So toast to the spheres that twinkle and play,
In a universe full of whimsy and sway.
Let's dance among the lights above,
In the vastness, we're all made of love!

Ocean of Storms Below the Halo

Dive right into the stormy sea,
Where waves are big as your best tea.
Sipping chaos on a grand wave,
Surfers try to be quite brave.

Under halos, the fish play chess,
While mermaids sing, it's quite the mess.
Octopuses juggle just for laughs,
With coral reefs making goofy graphs.

Turtles wear hats, what a sight,
In this ocean, everything's bright.
Dolphins giggle, making a fuss,
While squids argue on who's got the bus.

So dip your toes and have a laugh,
In the ocean, there's always a chaff.
Where storms can't stay in one place long,
And every wave hums a quirky song!

Exiles of the Orbital Frontier

Floating high on the fringe of play,
Exiles smile in their own weird way.
Whispers travel through the void,
From alien friends who are just overjoyed.

Meteor showers rain down cheer,
With space pirates who drink warm beer.
Galaxies spin with silly grins,
Hoping to join in on the whims.

Asteroids nod as they take a stroll,
While rockets blast off with a roll.
Making friends with the cosmic dust,
In the orbital frontier, it's a must!

So let us dance where the stars align,
With laughter echoing, feeling fine.
In the void, we write our tale,
On cosmic waves, we all set sail!

Tides of the Celestial Sea

Waves of stars crash on lunar shores,
With cosmic popcorn and silly roars.
Time is a loop, a rubber band,
In the tides of the vast, strange land.

Galaxies laugh, it's a hoot,
Cosmic crabs in a starry suit.
They shuffle around in their giggly dance,
While planets swish in their swirling pants.

Comets ride on surfboards too,
Sharing secrets, oh how they flew.
Constellations play hide and seek,
In the sea of stars, it's quite the freak.

So join the tides, let's float away,
In the celestial sea, we laugh and play.
Where stardust settles like confetti,
And every moment is warm and ready!

Beautiful Chaos in the Cosmic Canvas

In a swirl of stars, I lose my way,
A comet's tail just sprayed my toupee!
The planets giggle, they dance in the night,
I trip, I stumble, oh what a sight!

Jupiter's got a storm that never ends,
A cosmic party with zany friends.
Each time I skip, a moon takes a leap,
The laughter echoing, it's simply deep.

I paint my dreams with strokes of delight,
While galaxies twirl, oh what a flight!
A cosmic canvas, so wild, so bright,
Even black holes can't dim this light!

With Saturn's rings, I juggle and play,
They whisper secrets, then float away.
In beautiful chaos, here I reside,
A merry wanderer through stars that glide.

Symphonies of the Astral Tides

Pluto hums softly in chilly embrace,
While Mercury zips in a dizzying race.
Venus throws shade, but Mars bakes a pie,
They sing cosmic tunes as they float by.

Uranus grins wide with a glimmer of glee,
"Who needs gravity?" it laughs, "Just float with me!"
The waves of the stars play a hilarious song,
I dance on the rings, can't do much wrong!

Neptune's got secrets in watery blues,
Throwing astrological parties with mismatched shoes.
Every turn of a planet brings a new vibe,
Too cosmic to ponder, too bright to describe!

As meteors rock out with shimmering light,
Every twinkle and sparkle feels just so right.
In symphonies vast, with laughter and cheer,
The astral tides sing, we've nothing to fear!

Shadows in the Eternal Orbit

In shadows that dance through the void, I roam,
A pixelated nebula, my quirky home.
This orbit's a circus of odd little things,
With aliens teasing and jostling springs.

Orbiting Saturn, they play hide and seek,
With Saturnine winks and comical squeaks.
I trip over stardust, tumble and roll,
Blasting in laughter, that's the cosmic goal!

Asteroids chuckle, they juke to the left,
While Venus and Mars plot a spacey theft.
In shadows of mystery, hilarity reigns,
As laughter expands through these celestial chains.

The cosmos is wild, an eternal jest,
With echoes of joy, it's simply the best.
So here in the shadows, let's laugh and insist,
In the orb of the stars, it's the humor we missed!

Cadences of Saturnine Dreams

In dreams of a ringed planet's gallant embrace,
I dance with a moon, a whimsical chase.
Stars throw confetti, like it's a grand ball,
While comets come crashing, oh what a fall!

Waltzing in stardust, we laugh and we spin,
With echoes of giggles, let the fun begin!
The saturnine cadence keeps tripping my feet,
While Martians in tuxedos bring snacks, what a treat!

Shooting stars flash and dazzle my sight,
"Catch me if you can!" they gleefully write.
I chase their bright tails, but where do they lead?
To tickles of laughter through galaxies freed!

In Saturn's embrace, dreams twist and collide,
With jovial chants from each planetary side.
The universe winks, with humor supreme,
In the cadences bright of these saturnine dreams.

Fables Beneath the Cosmic Arch

In a land of gas and misty cheer,
Where space squirrels plot without fear.
They juggle moons, a daring stunt,
While comets cheer from their cosmic front.

Jupiter laughs, his belly round,
As Saturn's rings spin all around.
With wishes whispered to the stars,
They share their snacks from candy jars.

Aliens dance on fluffy clouds,
Wearing hats too big—oh, how proud!
Each twirl erupts in shining light,
As stardust sprinkles through the night.

So if you gaze, take note of fun,
For cosmic fables never shun.
Just look above with a gleeful grin,
The universe winks—let the laughter begin!

Notes from the Rings of Wonder

With rings like hula hoops they sway,
While space cats lounge in sunlight's play.
A note is dropped from Mars, you see,
It reads, 'I made a salad for thee!'

A dance party floats near bright Uranus,
Where odd-shaped beings sing with great fame,
They spin around in cosmic delight,
And galaxies giggle, oh what a sight!

Through playful whispers among the stars,
The universe bares its little scars.
Each twinkle holds a secret jest,
As planets gather for a fun-filled quest.

So tune your ears to the heavens' song,
For notes of joy linger all day long.
In the rings of wonder, life twirls wide,
Funny stories echo, let laughter be your guide!

Reflections on Ethereal Paths

Upon the paths of whirl and spin,
Cosmic mirrors invite you in.
Reflecting dreams, both silly and grand,
With a rainbow twist and a sandman's hand.

A careful stroll where stardust glows,
You might find wizards in funny clothes.
Casting spells that make you giggle,
Creating rainbows that wiggle and wiggle.

In the dance of planets, a bubble pops,
Jupiter's jokes make everyone stop.
With laughter ringing across the spheres,
Reflecting humor that spans the years.

So wade through pathways of cosmic fun,
With giggles echoing from sun to sun.
Join the jesters with their gleeful dash,
In the ethereal light, let your worries crash!

Chronicles of the Interstellar Breeze

A breeze blows soft through the cosmic tree,
Where wishful kittens chase wild debris.
Sailing on starlight, they twirl and prance,
Sharing secrets with a joyful glance.

Martian crabs in bow ties strut,
In interstellar games, they never shut.
Racing comets, they aim for the win,
Shouting 'Hooray!' with a cheeky grin.

Moonbeams tickle the shepherd's pie,
As space frogs leap, soaring high.
In this breeze of laughter and cheer,
All the silly antics bring love near.

So if you drift on the cosmic air,
Embrace the joy, shed every care.
For chronicles of laughter will never cease,
In the interstellar breeze, find your peace!

Cosmic Reflections

In the sky, there's twinkling cheese,
Planets waltz like playful bees.
Stars are laughing, can't you see?
Galaxies spinning, full of glee.

Rockets zoom, with silly tunes,
Asteroids dance under the moons.
Nebulas giggle, what a sight!
Comets chuckle through the night.

Aliens drop by for a chat,
Wearing hats and fancy pat.
Jokes about black holes draw a crowd,
Laughter echoes, bright and loud.

So when you gaze at night's parade,
Remember: cosmic jokes are made.
In this vast and funny space,
Laughter's found in every place.

The Symphony of the Cosmos

A grand orchestra plays up above,
Stars strum strings, in playful love.
Jupiter hits drums, oh what fun,
While Saturn spins, shining like the sun.

Planets sing in harmony bright,
Even comets join in the flight.
Black holes whistle a haunting tune,
While moons dance under a glowing moon.

The nebula hums a colorful beat,
All cosmic creatures join in, oh sweet!
Celestial giggles resonate wide,
As stardust flows like a joyous tide.

So turn up the stars and feel the vibe,
In this cosmic symphony, come and subscribe.
Let laughter echo through galaxies far,
For the cosmos is where we are.

Fragments of Celestial Dreams

In the night sky, dreams take flight,
Shooting stars with jokes so bright.
Aliens sketch on cosmic beams,
Drawing laughter in splintered dreams.

Planets gossip, what a sight,
Whirling around in pure delight.
Moons tell tales of wacky spins,
While suns shine bright with silly grins.

Cosmic kites in the stellar breeze,
Floating high with cosmic ease.
Gravity tickles the space-time cloth,
As laughter bursts from galactic broth.

So chase those dreams on deep space streams,
Laugh with the stars, let out your screams.
In every twinkle and ghostly gleam,
Are funny stories that boldly beam.

Orbiting Heartbeats

Planets orbit with rhythmic flair,
Each a heartbeat, light as air.
Moonbeams play a silly game,
While the sun laughs, calling their name.

Cosmic hearts in a jovial dance,
Falling stars take a playful chance.
Wobbling comets twirl in space,
Bringing smiles to every face.

Astro-bunnies hop around,
On rings of Saturn, they're tightly bound.
In this playful cosmic ballet,
Joyful jesters lead the way.

So feel the pulse of the universe,
In orbiting heartbeats, it's diverse.
With every giggle and cosmic sigh,
Love loops around as we fly high.

Ode to the Loyal Moons

Oh moons that spin around their lord,
In circles wide, never bored.
They wear their craters like a hat,
And giggle loud at every spat.

From Titan's giggles, wide and grand,
To tiny Mimas, shy and bland.
They play hide-and-seek in the dark,
Lighting up space with their spark.

But watch them closely, what a sight,
They trip on rings in the starry night.
With every tumble, they just grin,
In this cosmic dance, they all win.

So raise a toast to the moonlit crew,
With ice cream moons and skies so blue.
In their silly waltz around the sphere,
They spread pure joy, casting out fear.

Celestial Manuscripts in the Sky

Look up to the heavens, a cosmic book,
With tales of planets, take a look!
In handwritten ink of stardust bright,
They scribble secrets, day and night.

Jupiter's tales, tall and grand,
Wrapped in storms, they weave and stand.
While Venus winks with a fiery glow,
Scribbling her gossip, oh what a show!

Mars strikes poses, trying to flex,
With dusty secrets, oh, what a vex!
As Saturn laughs with a ringed applause,
In the library of skies, what a cause!

So gather 'round, oh starry fans,
Watch comets write with sparkly plans.
In this skyward script, laughter thrives,
As the universe quips and jives.

The Dance of Celestial Bodies

Planets pirouette in a cosmic spree,
With glittering orbits, oh so free!
They twirl and spin, a joyful delight,
Painting the cosmos with colors bright.

Saturn leads with his rings held high,
While Neptune floats by with a dreamy sigh.
Mars juggles moons, trying not to spill,
And Venus giggles with a charming thrill.

Asteroids tumble, a clumsy parade,
Rolling through space, making a shade.
Comets rush in, a swift little dash,
Leaving behind a sparkly flash.

So let us join this stellar dance,
In rhythm of gravity, take a chance.
With smiles so wide and hearts in tune,
We'll echo the laughs of the joyful moon.

Ballads in the Eye of the Storm

In storms of gas and swirling might,
The planets sing, oh what a sight!
With winds that howl and clouds that play,
They hum their ballads night and day.

Neptune croons in bluesy tone,
While Jupiter barks like a squeaky bone.
Uranus sways with its chilly flair,
Singing silly tunes to the cosmic air.

Through thunderous laughter, the asteroids cheer,
As they bounce through chaos, never fear.
And Saturn spins tales in the wildest gale,
In the eye of the storm, a joyful tale.

So here's to the ballads, funny and bright,
In the tempest's heart, we take flight.
With echoes of laughter, we'll make our way,
In this cosmic concert, come what may!

Dreams Beneath the Frozen Halo

In a land where penguins dance,
Frosty dreams take a silly stance.
Snowflakes hold a laughing spree,
Frosty jokes like cups of tea.

Marshmallow clouds float on air,
As polar bears perform with flair.
A comet slips on ice, oh dear,
With a twirl, it sheds a tear.

Jokes spun from the aurora's glow,
Tickling stars in a tasty show.
Cosmic giggles echo and ring,
Planets bounce and start to sing.

So come join the frosty jest,
Make a snowman in a vest.
With frozen smiles, we shall play,
In dreams that dance and sway all day.

Conversations with Celestial Shadows

In the dark, shadows converse,
Silly whispers, oh so terse.
Stars eavesdrop with brimming glee,
What do you hide, oh galaxy?

The moon winks with a cheeky grin,
While asteroids play tag, they spin.
Meteorites blush with much delight,
Always ready for a cosmic fight.

"Why's the sun always so bright?"
"Because it gets too much daylight!"
Laughter floats in the void of night,
As comets burst forth with pure delight.

So linger low, hear their tales,
As starlit giggles ride the gales.
In a universe full of jest,
Celestial banter can't be bested.

Journeys Through the Ice-Laden Abyss

Down we slide through crystal streets,
With frozen boots and frosty feasts.
Penguins waddle, trying to steer,
Cackling at the chill they fear.

"Hold on tight!" the starlight beams,
As they tumble through velvety dreams.
A spaceship made of candy cane,
Launches forth amidst the gain.

Ticklish winds take us so high,
While ice swans giggle as they fly.
Embrace the fridge of the unknown,
In glacial realms we all have grown.

So come along, bring laughs that shine,
In frosty depths, we intertwine.
Through the laughter, let's not miss,
The icy joy, a winter's kiss.

Serenade of the Starlit Sphere

In the dark, the stars arise,
Twinkling tunes, oh what a surprise.
With glittery voices, they sing aloud,
Jokes wrapped in laughter, cosmic and proud.

Planets spin in a merry dance,
Doing the cha-cha in a trance.
A comet tap-dances, quick on its feet,
Giving the universe a rhythmic treat.

"Oh dear, did you hear that star?
It said it dreams of being bizarre!"
Giggles escape from the Milky Way,
A serenade in a silly display.

So join the fun, let your heart soar,
In a sphere of laughter, there's always more.
With every chuckle, every cheer,
The starlit serenade draws us near.

www.ingramcontent.com/pod-product-compliance
Lightning Source LLC
Chambersburg PA
CBHW071838160426
43209CB00003B/335